BIG
BEASTS
Hippo

Stephanie
Turnbull

Published by Smart Apple Media,
an imprint of Black Rabbit Books
P.O. Box 3263, Mankato, Minnesota, 56002
www.blackrabbitbooks.com

Designed by Hel James
Edited by Mary-Jane Wilkins

Library of Congress Cataloging-in-Publication Data
Turnbull, Stephanie.
    Hippo / Stephanie Turnbull.
        pages cm. -- (Big beasts)
    Summary: "Describes the characteristics of Hippos
and their life and habitat"-- Provided by publisher.
    Audience: K to Grade 3.
    Includes index.
    ISBN 978-1-62588-165-6
    1. Hippopotamus--Juvenile literature. I. Title.
QL737.U57T87 2015
599.63'5--dc23
                        2014003968

Photo acknowledgements
l = left, r = right, t = top, b = bottom
title Eric Isselee/Shutterstock; page 3 Anup Shah/Thinkstock;
4 iStockphoto/Thinkstock; 6 Roadworks, 7 iStockphoto/
both Thinkstock; 9 Dr_Flash/Shutterstock; 10 Tom Brakefield/
Thinkstock; 11 Steffen Foerster/Shutterstock; 12 Elizevh,
13 Stu Porter/both Shutterstock; 14 Mark O'Flaherty/Shutterstock;
15 Jupiterimages/Thinkstock; 17 Sam DCruz/Thinkstock;
18 J Reineke/Shutterstock; 20 Piotr Gatlik, 21 Dennis Donohue/
both Shutterstock; 22t sababa66/Shutterstock, bl Keith Levit
Photography, br iStockphoto/both Thinkstock; 23t Sergey
Uryadnikov, b PdaMai/both Shutterstock
Cover Eric Isselee/Shutterstock

Printed in China

DAD0059
032014
9 8 7 6 5 4 3 2 1

Contents

Hippos are
enormous!

3

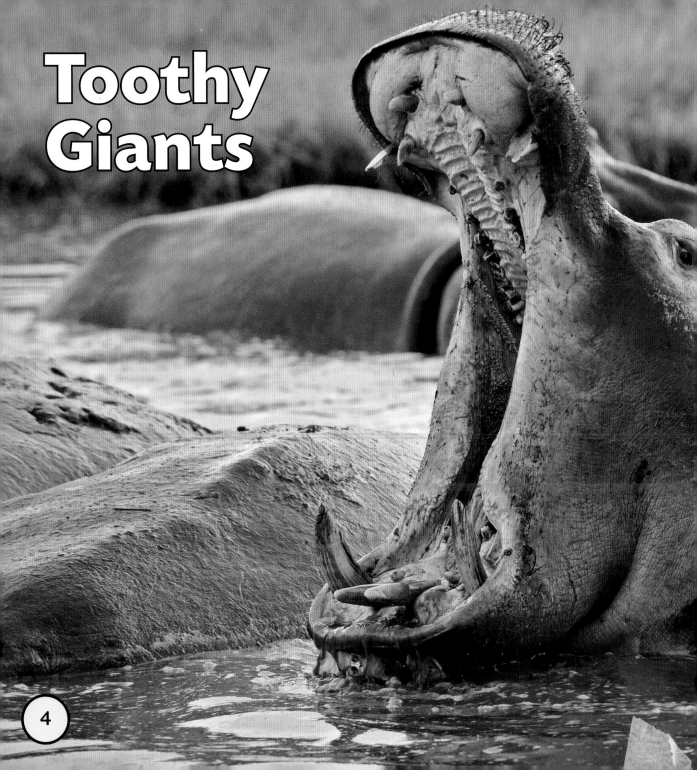

Toothy Giants

Hippos are one
of the biggest land
animals in the world.

A hippo has a
barrel-shaped body,
stubby legs...

... and a **massive
mouth** that opens
e x t r a - w i d e.

The two longest teeth
are often called tusks.

Keeping Cool

Hippos spend their days wallowing in muddy African lakes and rivers. This keeps them cool and from burning in the hot sun.

An oily red liquid oozes out of their skin and acts as a sun block. Can you see the red droplets?

Lying Low

Hippos love to lie on shallow river beds, almost completely covered in water.

A hippo's eyes, ears, and nostrils are high on its head, so it can still see, hear, and breathe when it's almost underwater.

Under the Water

Sometimes hippos sink to the bottom of deep rivers and walk along the bottom, pushing off with wide, webbed toes.

They can hold their breath underwater for five minutes, then pop up for air with a *WHOOSH* of spray.

Big Families

Hippos live in family groups of around 15 animals. These are mostly females, babies, and young hippos.

Each group has one huge male leader. He guards the family and the stretch of river where they live.

Stay Away!

Male leaders are grumpy, vicious, and afraid of nothing!

They chase and attack animals who dare to come near their territory.

Beware! Hippos sprint faster than a human, and their mighty jaws can crush a crocodile.

Brutal Battles

Sometimes another male tries to take over as leader. This leads to a big fight!

First, the males open their mouths wide, each trying to look the biggest.

Then they *lunge* at each other, biting, bellowing, and thrashing.

They wrestle violently until one gives up—or is killed.

Dinner Time

Hippos may be ferocious creatures,
but they only eat grass.

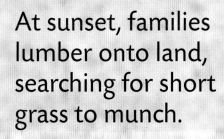

At sunset, families
lumber onto land,
searching for short
grass to munch.

They graze for a few
hours, then plop
back into the water
before sunrise.

Hippo Babies

Hippo calves are born
in water, so they must learn
to swim right away!

They stay close to their mother and drink her milk.
Mothers watch out for animals such as crocodiles
and lions, who may attack babies.

BIG Facts

Adult hippos are about 14 feet (4m) long.

The only land animals bigger than hippos are elephants and rhinos.

A newborn calf weighs ten times more than a human baby.

Hippo skin is as thick as a pile of 15 of these books.

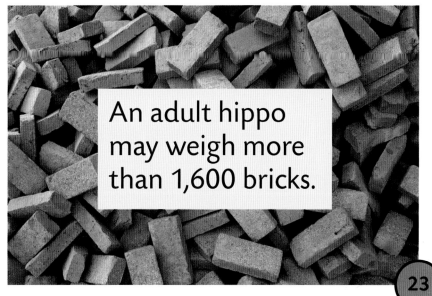

An adult hippo may weigh more than 1,600 bricks.

Useful Words

calf
The name for a baby hippo.

territory
The stretch of water where a hippo family lives. Male hippos guard their territory fiercely.

tusks
A hippo's two extra-long front teeth, used for fighting.

Index

Web Link

Visit this web site for hippo facts and photos:
www.nationalgeographic.com/kids/animals/creature feature/hippopotamus